DESERT DREAMINGS

DEIRDRE STOKES

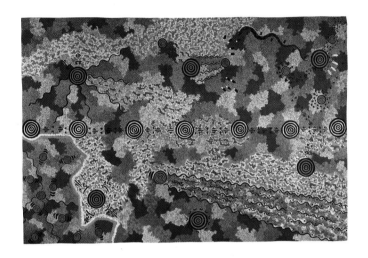

Rigby

Contents

The Dreamtime

Aboriginal people believe in a creation time, or Dreamtime, when ancestral beings emerged from beneath the earth. They resembled plants and animals, but were part-human.

Journeying across the land, the ancestors created everything that formed the world. They behaved like human beings — hunting, fighting, loving and hating. They taught their descendants the sacred rituals and the symbols and designs used in body painting.

The ancestors were the law makers and from their deeds Aboriginal people learnt the correct way to behave and to live with each other.

As these mythical creatures tired of their life they disappeared under the earth again. Often these places are marked by rocky outcrops and trees and so have special religious significance to Aboriginal people.

Tjukurpa is an Aboriginal word which we interpret as the Dreamtime. To Aborigines, the Tjukurpa means existence in the past, present and future.

In the beginning

The Aborigines' nomadic way of life and the extremes of the desert climate made it unlikely that much of their art would be preserved. Designs painted on artefacts quickly wore off. Body paint and sand mosaics were only intended to last for the duration of the ceremony.

Today, however, great care is taken to preserve and record Aboriginal art. It is recognised as an important part of our heritage.

Rock engraving

Rock engraving is the oldest and most lasting form of traditional Aboriginal art and is found in most parts of Australia where there are suitable rock surfaces.

Many different methods were used. These include rubbing, scratching, drilling and pitting. Stone, wooden or other implements were used, depending on the texture of the rock.

These rock engravings, about 100 kilometres south of Alice Springs, are believed to be thousands of years old. They include circles, arcs, lines, and bird and animal tracks.

Rock painting

In the desert areas of Central and South Australia the designs in rock painting are similar to those used in rock engraving.

The Aboriginal artists used natural pigments — white from pipe clay or gypsum, red and yellow ochres from the earth and black from charcoal or manganese.

The pigments were ground to a powder and mixed with a natural glue, then applied with the fingers or a

brush. Brushes might be made from a chewed twig, strips of bark or human hair, depending on the surface to be covered.

Often, drawings were made with a small stone and then paint was rubbed on with the hand. Paint might also be splattered onto rock walls or a stencilled design made by blowing paint over an object such as a hand.

Sand drawings

Sand drawings can depict objects, illustrate a story, or be a map of the landscape, indicating landmarks and distances to be travelled.

Ground mosaics

Ground mosaics are made from the finely chopped leaves, stems and flowers of the native daisy and birds' feathers. The pulp is rubbed in animal fat. Half is then dyed with powdered yellow or red ochre or human blood, the other half with powdered white clay or black charcoal, and formed into small pellets.

A piece of ground is cleared and flattened, and spread with crumbled termite mound to give a hard working surface. The coloured pellets are placed side-by-side to create the design.

The mosaics are usually part of a religious ceremony. Sometimes they include a ceremonial pole in the centre. The mosaics are destroyed by the dancing during the ceremony. Only ground mosaics of a non-sacred nature can be photographed.

Body painting

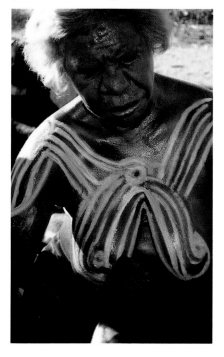

Body painting is a group activity associated with various ceremonies. The painting begins several hours before the ceremony and is accompanied by singing to call on the spiritual powers of the ancestral beings.

The body is first greased. Then the traditional designs are applied with the index finger and painting sticks. The materials used are red ochre, black charcoal and white clay.

This woman's body is being painted for a ceremony.

Painting on artefacts

Throughout the Western Desert there is an important tradition of wood carving. For many generations, water carriers, spear throwers, boomerangs and other articles have been superbly carved and painted. The designs used are similar to those in body decoration, ground mosaics and sand drawings.

Water carriers and other wooden artefacts are painted with designs that tell a story.

A hidden message

Aboriginal art uses traditional symbols which can be read in many ways. Because of this, even the secret, sacred parts of a Dreaming can be painted but still remain hidden from us. The artist is the only person who fully understands the meaning.

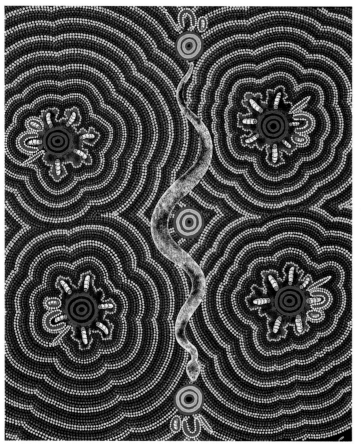

Mary Dixon Nungurrayi
Warlpiri
Witchetty Grub Dreaming
92 × 76 cm

This painting is associated with the Witchetty Grub Dreaming site of Kunatjarrayi to the north-west of Papunya. The painting depicts women, represented by "U" shapes, gathering witchetty grubs from the roots of trees with their digging sticks and wooden bowls. As they dig, one of the grubs turns into a snake and travels north towards the Granites. At a deeper level, a parallel can be drawn between the witchetty grub turning into a moth and a boy's initiation into manhood.

Symbols of desert art

These are some of the traditional symbols used in desert art. They have many different interpretations; only a few of their meanings are given.

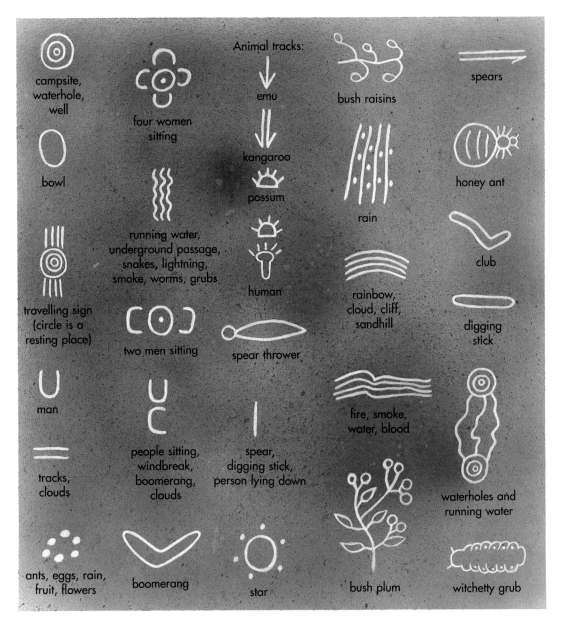

campsite, waterhole, well

bowl

travelling sign (circle is a resting place)

man

tracks, clouds

ants, eggs, rain, fruit, flowers

four women sitting

running water, underground passage, snakes, lightning, smoke, worms, grubs

two men sitting

people sitting, windbreak, boomerang, clouds

boomerang

Animal tracks:

emu

kangaroo

possum

human

spear thrower

spear, digging stick, person lying down

star

spears

bush raisins

rain

rainbow, cloud, cliff, sandhill

fire, smoke, water, blood

bush plum

honey ant

club

digging stick

waterholes and running water

witchetty grub

Looking at desert art

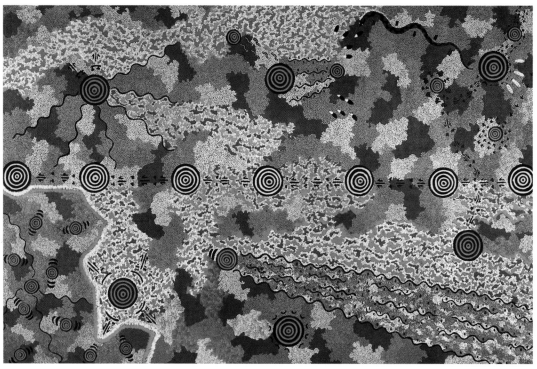

Michael Nelson Tjakamarra (born 1949)
Warlpiri
Papunya, N.T.
Dreaming sites in the Western Desert

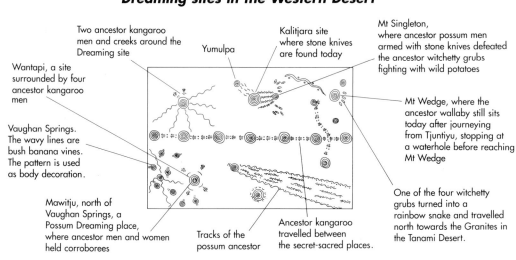

Two ancestor kangaroo men and creeks around the Dreaming site

Yumulpa

Kalitjara site where stone knives are found today

Mt Singleton, where ancestor possum men armed with stone knives defeated the ancestor witchetty grubs fighting with wild potatoes

Wantapi, a site surrounded by four ancestor kangaroo men

Mt Wedge, where the ancestor wallaby still sits today after journeying from Tjuntiyu, stopping at a waterhole before reaching Mt Wedge

Vaughan Springs. The wavy lines are bush banana vines. The pattern is used as body decoration.

Mawitju, north of Vaughan Springs, a Possum Dreaming place, where ancestor men and women held corroborees

Tracks of the possum ancestor

Ancestor kangaroo travelled between the secret-sacred places.

One of the four witchetty grubs turned into a rainbow snake and travelled north towards the Granites in the Tanami Desert.

Dots in Aboriginal art

The use of dots in modern Aboriginal paintings comes from rock painting, body painting and ground designs (sand drawings and ground mosaics).

The coloured patterns of dots, side-by-side or dot-on-dot, create three-dimensional pictures full of life and movement.

Dots may also represent the landscape. When viewed from a high point or from the air, the country often appears dotted with low scrub, clumps of spinifex, trees, sandhills and rocky outcrops. The scene to the

left is a good example of this; and if you look closely at the bottom right of the photo you will see an Aboriginal "sand drawing" made with different colours of gravel.

In these two modern paintings, patterns of dots are used to represent traditional stories. The picture on the left depicts a food-gathering story. The women (who traditionally collect bush tucker) are shown by the "U" shapes; the long thin shapes are the digging sticks; and the ovals are the wooden dishes in which the foods are placed. The one on the right tells the story of a budgerigar spirit ancestor. The wavy line is the bird's travels through desert country between waterholes.

Stories of the Dreamtime

The stories of the ancestral journeys tell about the landscape, animal habits, social laws and customs, and religious beliefs.

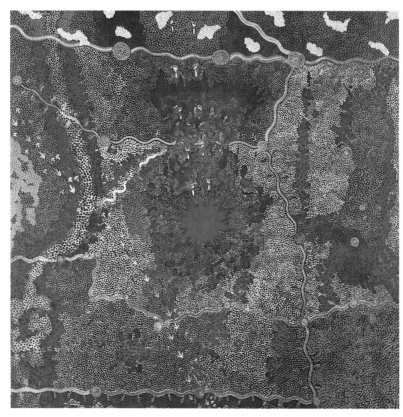

Clifford Possum Tjapaltjarri, assisted by his brother, **Tim Leura Tjapaltjarri**
Anmatyerre/Arrernte
Papunya N.T.
Warlugulong, 1976
synthetic polymer paint on canvas
Purchased 1981
Art Gallery of
New South Wales

Clifford Possum Tjapaltjarri
with members of his family

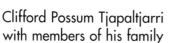

The painting *Warlugulong* is like an aerial map of the artist's country, depicting the journeys of Dreamtime ancestors and teaching social law and custom.

The central story of this painting is of Lungkata the Blue-tongue Lizard Man whose two sons, while out hunting, speared a kangaroo. Feeling very hungry, they decided to cook and eat it themselves, instead of sharing it with their father as the law demands.

Lungkata grew suspicious about their long absence and, when he realised what had happened, decided to punish them immediately for breaking the law.

Blowing on his firestick until it glowed, he set light to a dry bush which exploded into flame. Tongues of flame flicked out like the tongue of the blue-tongue lizard and raced across the land.

A blue-tongue lizard

Very quickly the flames caught up with the two sons. They tried to beat out the flames with tree branches, but it was useless. However fast they ran, the fire followed them.

Finally exhausted, they could run no longer and the flames overwhelmed them.

New materials, traditional stories

In the early 1970s a new development in Aboriginal art took place at Papunya School, Northern Territory. Aboriginal pupils were encouraged to paint murals on the walls in their traditional designs, using acrylic paints.

This mural on the school walls tells how the Honey Ant Spirit Beings travelled out of the west towards eastern Australia and held a major meeting at Papunya.

The children's work remained unfinished but several of the older men in the community completed the project.

Soon, many Aboriginal artists began to paint their Dreamings in acrylic paints on canvas or any available scrap material.

At Yuendumu, N.T., the older men then decided to paint their traditional stories on the school doors. Their children were being taught white ways and had no knowledge of the Dreaming stories or Aboriginal laws and customs. This was a way that they could learn. Two of the doors are shown on the facing page.

Acrylic paints are ideal for the hot dusty desert conditions. They only need to be thinned with water, they are quick drying and permanent and can be applied with any kind of implement.

This door tells the story of two men with spears, spear-throwers and other weapons, who hunted for kangaroos and other animals. The painting also shows their home.

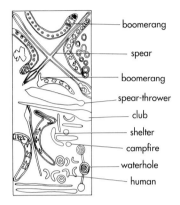

- boomerang
- spear
- boomerang
- spear-thrower
- club
- shelter
- campfire
- waterhole
- human

This painting on this door shows the Yam and Bush Tomato Dreamings at a place west of Yuendumu.

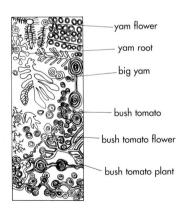

- yam flower
- yam root
- big yam
- bush tomato
- bush tomato flower
- bush tomato plant

Where the desert artists li

Each group has its own territory. The features of the landscape and sacred sites created by the mythical ancestors are important in every aspect of life.

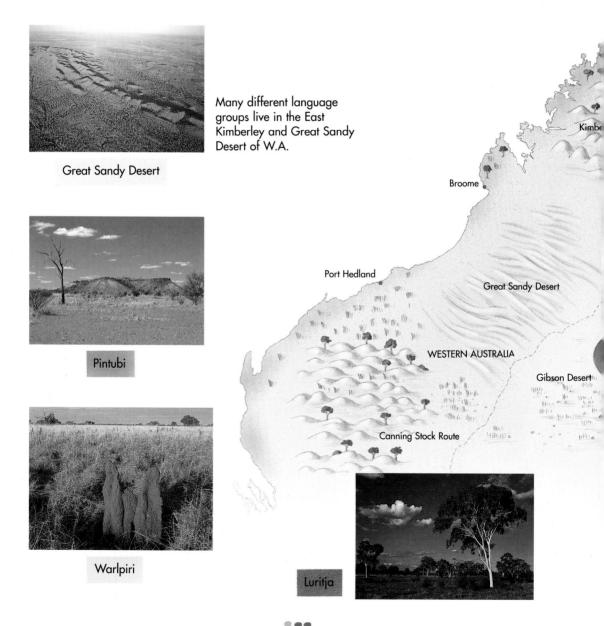

Great Sandy Desert

Many different language groups live in the East Kimberley and Great Sandy Desert of W.A.

Pintubi

Warlpiri

Luritja

Kimbe

Broome

Port Hedland

Great Sandy Desert

WESTERN AUSTRALIA

Gibson Desert

Canning Stock Route

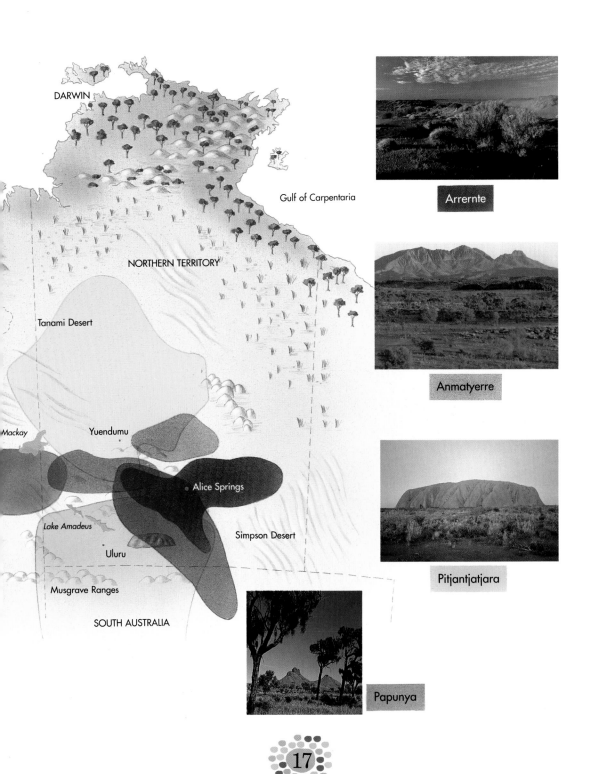

DARWIN

Gulf of Carpentaria

NORTHERN TERRITORY

Tanami Desert

Mackay

Yuendumu

Alice Springs

Lake Amadeus

Simpson Desert

Uluru

Musgrave Ranges

SOUTH AUSTRALIA

Arrernte

Anmatyerre

Pitjantjatjara

Papunya

The paintings, the land and the people

The paintings are a visual record of the Dreamings, and they explain the artist's relationship to the land. In the mind of the artist, the land is mapped out with Dreaming trails and the features created by the mythical ancestors.

Artist Michael Nelson Tjakamarra with one of his paintings. See how the painting reflects the colours and appearance of the landscape.

Canvases may be painted by one artist, by a husband and wife, or by a number of men or women of the same kinship group.

The artists, as they paint, sing the stories which explain the meanings of the symbols they are using.

Two Warlpiri women, Noreen and Doris Nungerrayi, paint their Witchetty Grub Dreaming.

Valerie Kemarre
Bush Cucumber Vine, 1989
Synthetic polymer on linen
150 × 120.5 cm

These vines only grow after heavy rain. The vine depicted here is covered in fruit.

Different places, different styles

There is such a deep personal bond between the artist and the land that variations in the landscape have a strong influence on the style of the art. In the vast desert areas the landscape varies considerably, and this is reflected in the art.

These paintings are by artists living in different parts of the east Kimberley region in the north of Western Australia. Each has a distinctive way of depicting the landscape and the Dreamings associated with it.

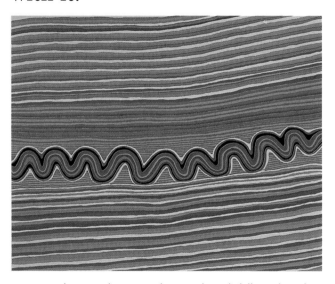

Jimmy Pike (born c. 1940)
Walmajarri
Kurlku, Great Sandy Desert, W.A.
Yarntayi with jilji on both sides

Jimmy Pike was born and spent his childhood in the remote sandhill country of the Great Sandy Desert. His family lived a semi-nomadic life moving from one waterhole to another within their own country. He is an expert at hunting and tracking, and knows every feature of the landscape.

This painting tells the Dreamtime story of the creation of Yarntayi. Two giant snakes travelled through the country, cutting a sinuous path from east to west. They pushed aside the jilji or long rolling sandhills to leave wide, flat, treeless plains between them.

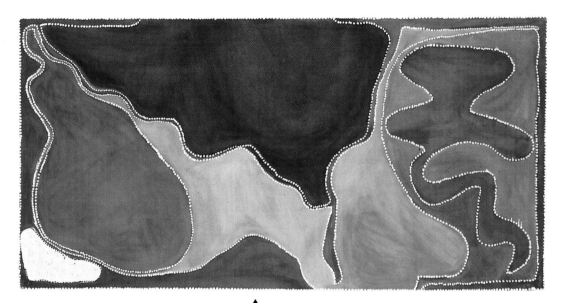

▲
Rover Thomas (born c. 1935)
Kukatja/Wangkajungka
Turkey Creek — Warnum, W.A.
Bedford Downs Massacre, 1987
Natural pigments and bush gum on cotton duck
89.5 × 180.5 cm

Rover Thomas's paintings are a visual record of the significance of the Kimberley landscape to the Aboriginal people. They include recent features such as roads, towns and cattle stations. This painting commemorates a massacre of Aborigines that took place in the early days of European settlement.

◀**David Jarinyanu Downs** (born c. 1925)
Wankajungu/Walmajarri
Fitzroy Crossing, W.A.
Kurtal as Miltjitawurru, 1989
Natural ochres and synthetic polymer on linen
183 × 122 cm

This painting explains the origin of a weather pattern which brings dramatic rain storms to the Kimberleys in December. These storms, called Miltjitawurru, herald the beginning of the wet season, and give relief from stifling heat.

In the painting Kurtal is depicted carrying the rain clouds and surrounded by them. Kurtal as Miltjitawurru can destroy animals and people in his path, but he also creates life by making the dry earth fertile again.

A mixture of old and new

For thousands of years, desert Aborigines have slept out under clear, star-studded skies. So it is not surprising that there are so many Dreamtime creation myths explaining the origins of the sun, moon, stars and planets.

These two paintings by Warlpiri artists show contrasting techniques. Mary Dixon Nungurrayi uses traditional designs to depict a Dreamtime story; but because Aboriginal art is part of a living culture Bronson Nelson Jakamarra has introduced new symbols to help him depict a recent astronomical event.

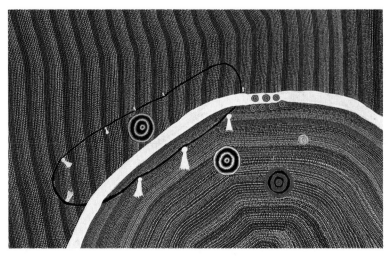

Bronson Nelson Jakamarra
Warlpiri
Yuendumu, N.T.
Halley's Comet, 1986
Synthetic polymer paint on canvas
78 × 126 cm

The artist was inspired by a technical drawing in a magazine illustrating the path of Halley's Comet. The painting shows the comet at various stages as it circles the sun. The other planets, depicted as circles, are the Earth, the moon, the Pleiades (Seven Sisters) and Venus. The white band is the Milky Way and the dots are the stars. The Milky Way and the Pleiades are important Dreamings for the Warlpiri people.

Mary Dixon Nungurrayi
Warlpiri
Mt Liebig area, N.T.
The Seven Sisters
Dreaming
Synthetic polymer paint on
canvas
128.5 × 83 cm

In the Dreamtime seven young Aboriginal girls were looking for honey ants at Uluru. An old man, Jilbi, saw them and decided to steal two of them to become his wives. During the night he followed them across the desert, but to save them the Spirit Beings at Uluru put the seven girls into the sky to form the Seven Sister stars or Pleiades. Jilbi was put into the sky as the star Orion. He still continues his pursuit as he follows the sisters across the night sky.

The painting depicts the Seven Sisters, the stars of the night sky and the Milky Way. Surrounding these are the designs and colours of the body painting worn by the women during a very important ceremony connected with this story.

Traditional knowledge aids scientific research

Today Aboriginal people and scientists using modern research techniques are working together to record age-old knowledge about medicinal plants. They are recording the healing properties of thousands of species of plants used by Aboriginal people since ancient times, and the traditions associated with them.

Mick Namerari Tjapaltjarri
(born c. 1926)
Pintubi
Papunya (then Kintore), N.T.
Medicine Story, 1972
Acrylic on canvas
76.2 × 61 cm

Because of his concern for the health of the young men at the Pintubi camp, Mick Tjapaltjarri painted this "medicine story". It was the first canvas painted at Papunya, inspired by the need to teach the young men the traditional ways for good healthy living which were being ignored in the camp.

The painting depicts four corroboree men dancing and chanting to "keep the kids alive". Above them is a large plant spreading across the desert, above it two "kids alive". In the lower sections are the roots of nutritious bush tucker pushing through the earth.

There is much ritual concerned with the collecting of plants for medicines, with special Dreamings to be sung to ensure the maximum medicinal value from the plants.

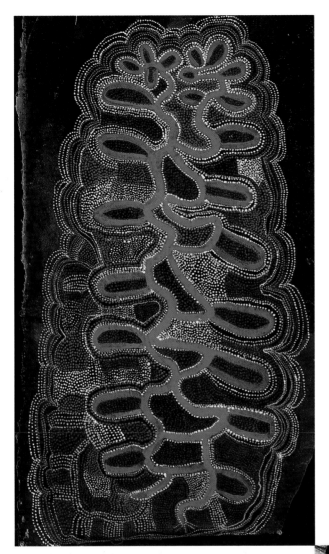

Louisa Napaljarri Lawson
(Pupiya) (born c. 1930)
Warlpiri
Lajamanu, N.T.
Medicine Vine (Ngalyipi) Dreaming, 1987
Acrylic on bark
125.5 × 73.5 cm (irregular)

Medicine vine, *Tinospora smilacina*

The artist has depicted the whole vine with its roots, stem, leaves, flowers and fruit. The woody stem curls around the trunks and branches of trees like a huge snake. It has creamy-white flowers, and the fruit is green, ripening to red.

This plant is a commonly used and effective bush medicine. The heated leaves draw poison from infected sores, relieve headaches when placed on the forehead, and cure a sore throat when chewed. The stem, when softened and pounded, makes a "sticky bandage".

Desert art in the city

Aboriginal art can now be seen in our capital city in a form in which it is both useful and permanent.

The granite mosaic pavement in the open forecourt of the new Parliament House in Canberra was designed by Michael Nelson Tjakamarra (see page 18). It represents our ancient continent and our oldest civilisation.

The Aboriginal meaning of the name Canberra is "meeting place", and the mosaic shows a gathering of tribespeople of the Dingo, Wallaby and Goanna ancestors for an important ceremony.

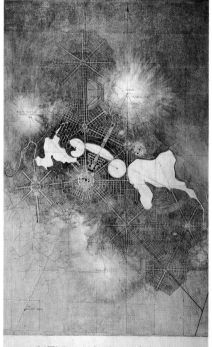

CITY AND ENVIRONS·

During the construction the artist worked with the mosaicists to make sure that his acrylic painting was accurately transformed into the final mosaic.

The design was marked out on large sheets of paper, and the setts — small roughly-finished pieces of granite — stuck in place on the paper (see photo top left).

The setts were put in place by turning over the completed sheets. They were then cemented down and set in a background of black mortar (see photo above).

The radial lines in the mosaic, together with those paved into the surrounding forecourt, form a link with Walter Burley Griffin's geometric design for our capital city. His original plan is shown on the left.

Traditional craft today

For thousands of years, the Aboriginal people have been making useful articles from natural materials around them. Like people in many other parts of the world, they have found ways of making these useful objects beautiful. Traditionally, Aboriginal craft work was intended for everyday use, not for display in museums and galleries. However, because the beauty of these objects has been recognised, many items are now housed where people can view them.

Arts and crafts centres have been set up, where craft work made in the settlements can be sold and distributed throughout Australia. This industry ensures that traditional skills are not lost, and provides income for the craftspeople and their families.

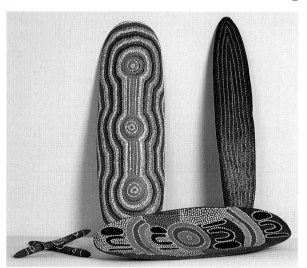 

These beautifully crafted wooden artefacts were made by Pitjantjatjara people. The desert animals, music sticks and bowls or coolamons are made by the women, while the men make the hunting weapons. The Pitjantjatjara women decorate their artefacts with hot pokerwork designs taken from body painting or depicting events from the Dreamings.

Designs for living

In recent times, Aboriginal art has become far more accessible to all Australians, but this has caused some problems for the artists. As their designs have become popular, these have sometimes been used without permission or acknowledgement. However, laws have now been passed to protect the rights of artists.

The items on this page demonstrate to the world that one of its oldest cultures is dynamic and living, open and adaptable to an ever-changing world.

How the artists work today

The success of Aboriginal art has brought to the artists both a feeling of pride in their achievements and a change in life style.

In the 1970s Aboriginal people in remote areas began leaving mission stations and government settlements to establish outstations. These are settlements where they can lead a more traditional life but still have access to community services and consumer goods.

Profits from the sale of traditional arts and crafts are an important source of income for these settlements. They have helped to fund the purchase of equipment — vehicles, generators, bulldozers, water tanks, for example. Artists share their profits with relatives and painting assistants. An artist may own a motor vehicle but it will be used by everyone in the family group. Artists and their families are able to drive to or charter aircraft to attend annual cultural festivals. Many travel interstate and overseas to exhibitions of their paintings.

This Napaljarri artist at Mt Allan, N.T., is painting the designs of sand drawings on canvas.

In December 1991 Clifford Possum Tjapaltjarri visited the Sheraton Ayers Rock Hotel at Yulara, and ran a painting workshop with students from the local school.

Warlpiri artist Topsy Napururrla of Yuendumu paints a carved wooden dish.

Aboriginal art reaches the world

Today people from all over the world are enjoying and purchasing Aboriginal art. Paintings are hung in our public art galleries and sold by art dealers. Large exhibitions of Aboriginal art have been held in New York, Paris and London. The two paintings on this page hang in the National Gallery of Victoria in Melbourne.

◀ **Sunfly Tjampitjin** (b. 1916)
Kukatja
Balgo Hills, W.A.
Tjikerri — near Lake Mackay, 1987
Acrylic on canvas
113 × 83 cm

Tjikerri is a sacred site for men. Warlayirti, the ancient leader of the Kukatja people, travelled here in the Dreaming. After a long journey from the north he lay down, forming the waterhole and lake shown at the top of the painting.

◀ **Peter Blacksmith Yapanangka**
Kartangarurru
Lajamanu, N.T.
Snake Dreaming, 1986
Acrylic and housepaint on composition board
110.5 × 210.4 cm

The painting tells the story of the powerful snake ancestor's journey in search of water. The snake's journey was followed by a rainbow, then by rain.